THE CENTER FOR PREVENTIVE ACTION

Nigeria

Elections and Continuing Challenges

Robert I. Rotberg

CSR NO. 27, APRIL 2007
COUNCIL ON FOREIGN RELATIONS

Founded in 1921, the Council on Foreign Relations is an independent, national membership organization and a nonpartisan center for scholars dedicated to producing and disseminating ideas so that individual and corporate members, as well as policymakers, journalists, students, and interested citizens in the United States and other countries, can better understand the world and the foreign policy choices facing the United States and other governments. The Council does this by convening meetings; conducting a wide-ranging Studies Program; publishing *Foreign Affairs*, the preeminent journal covering international affairs and U.S. foreign policy; maintaining a diverse membership; sponsoring Independent Task Forces and Special Reports; and providing up-to-date information about the world and U.S. foreign policy on the Council's website, CFR.org.

THE COUNCIL TAKES NO INSTITUTIONAL POSITION ON POLICY ISSUES AND HAS NO AFFILIATION WITH THE U.S. GOVERNMENT. ALL STATEMENTS OF FACT AND EXPRESSIONS OF OPINION CONTAINED IN ITS PUBLICATIONS ARE THE SOLE RESPONSIBILITY OF THE AUTHOR OR AUTHORS.

Council Special Reports (CSRs) are concise policy briefs, produced to provide a rapid response to a developing crisis or contribute to the public's understanding of current policy dilemmas. CSRs are written by individual authors—who may be Council Fellows or acknowledged experts from outside the institution—in consultation with an advisory committee, and are intended to take sixty days or less from inception to publication. The committee serves as a sounding board and provides feedback on a draft report. It usually meets twice—once before a draft is written and once again when there is a draft for review; however, advisory committee members, unlike Task Force members, are not asked to sign off on the report or to otherwise endorse it. Once published, CSRs are posted on the Council's website, CFR.org.

For further information about the Council or this Special Report, please write to the Council on Foreign Relations, 58 East 68th Street, New York, NY 10021, or call the Communications office at 212-434-9888. Visit our website, CFR.org.

To submit a letter in response to a Council Special Report for publication on our website, CFR.org, you may send an email to CSReditor@cfr.org. Alternatively, letters may be mailed to us at: Publications Department, Council on Foreign Relations, 58 East 68th Street, New York, NY 10021. Letters should include the writer's name, postal address, and daytime phone number. Letters may be edited for length and clarity, and may be published online. Please do not send attachments. All letters become the property of the Council on Foreign Relations and will not be returned. We regret that, owing to the volume of correspondence, we cannot respond to every letter.

CONTENTS

FOREWORD

Nigeria is Africa's most populous country, the home of sub-Saharan Africa's largest Muslim population, and one of the world's leading oil producers. While Nigeria has the potential to be a successful case study of economic and political reform and religious cooperation, it faces serious problems, including corruption, internal unrest, an HIV/AIDS epidemic, and a struggling economy. Nigeria, the United States, and the international community all have a vested interest in ensuring that the country addresses these challenges and becomes a peaceful, stable democracy. As Robert I. Rotberg details in the latest Council Special Report, a crucial step in this process is for Nigeria to conduct free, fair, and credible gubernatorial and national elections in April 2007.

Nigeria: Elections and Continuing Challenges, sponsored by the Council's Center for Preventive Action, suggests immediate and medium-term courses of action for Nigerians and members of the international community. Some of Rotberg's policy recommendations, such as election monitoring, are focused on helping Nigeria avoid a near-term breakdown of democracy. Others, such as strengthening health care infrastructure and improving security, look more broadly to the future and tackle the country's fundamental challenges of governance and development. As this report makes clear, the stakes are large: The upcoming elections will dramatically affect this critical country's prospects—which in turn will dramatically affect the future of all of Africa.

Richard N. Haass
President
Council on Foreign Relations
April 2007

PREFACE AND ACKNOWLEDGMENTS

Ever since its independence, Nigeria—big, bursting with energy and ideas, boastful, brusque, and bawdy—has known that the aspirations and hopes of Africa rested on its ample, restless shoulders. Today Nigeria, having survived decades of despotism and profligacy, is engaged strenuously in a critical exercise of nation-building. April's elections are a major component of that still to be completed project. Electing a president, 469 parliamentarians, thirty-six state governors, and all of the assemblymen in the thirty-six state legislatures will demonstrate how effectively Nigeria and Nigerians have entered a new era of accountable government and how the signal accomplishments of the Obasanjo administration have prepared firm foundations for the positive years to come. Or the election exercise will be flawed but still acceptable, and the stop-start maturation of an integrated, peaceful, developmentally insecure nation will continue in the mixed, hesitant manner in which it has begun.

Nigeria is beyond ready for a paradigm shift. This report suggests how far Nigeria has come, and the many tough tasks that lie ahead. It recommends immediate attention to Nigeria's needs and brisk action by Washington, and sets out challenges and opportunities for Nigerians and other powers. This report's recommendations call for general and specific attention to Nigeria's most pressing needs. Nigeria's welfare is fundamental to Africa's welfare. This report shows how and where insiders and outsiders can make a decisive difference.

This report was made possible in part by a grant from the Carnegie Corporation of New York and by the many individuals who have generously supported the work of the Center for Preventive Action. The report, which continues the excellent work of the center, follows on several of the Council's reports on crisis areas in Africa and flows intellectually and in a policy sense out of the work and findings of a significant Council Task Force, *More than Humanitarianism: A Strategic U.S. Approach Toward Africa*.

Princeton N. Lyman and William L. Nash, esteemed friends and colleagues, pressed me hard to write this report. I thank them for their confidence and their very constructive critiques of early drafts. Equally constructive and helpful in their oral and written critiques of early and subsequent drafts of the report were Johnnie Carson, Michelle D. Gavin, David L. Goldwyn, Howard F. Jeter, Darren Kew, Peter M. Lewis, Simeon Moats, and Rotimi Suberu. Richard N. Haass and Gary Samore also provided valuable comments on the report. I thank them all, and so should readers. This report, however, reflects the judgments and recommendations of the author only.

This report could not have been written without the research support of Heather Jensen and Debbie West, whose assistance I acknowledge with gratitude. Jamie A. Ekern held the report together from beginning to end. She deserves all of our thanks.

Robert I. Rotberg

MAP

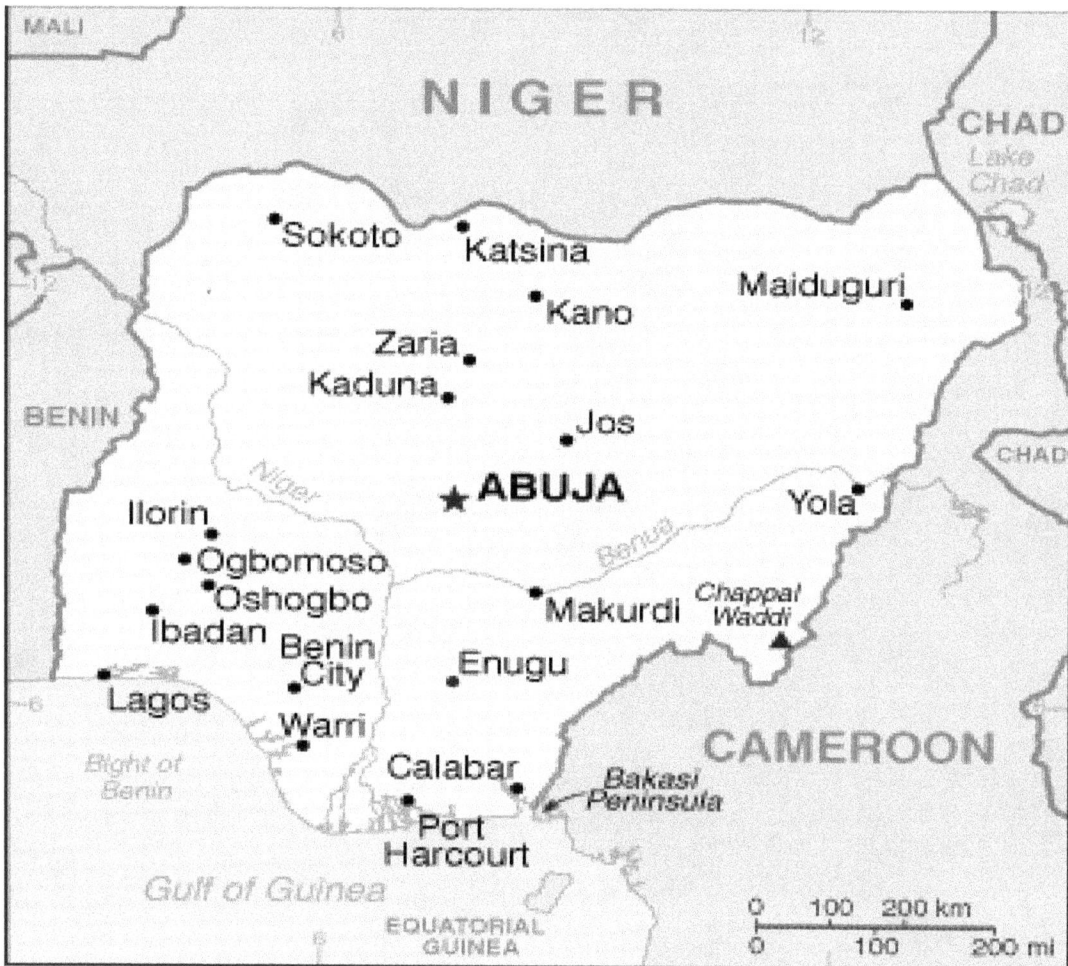

Source: Central Intelligence Agency World Factbook, https://www.cia.gov/cia/publications/factbook/geos/ni.html.

ACRONYMS

EFCC	Economic and Financial Crimes Commission
EU	European Union
GDP	gross domestic product
HDI	Human Development Index
ICITAP	International Criminal Investigation Training Assistance Program
IFES	International Foundation for Election Systems
INEC	Independent National Electoral Commission
IRI	International Republican Institute
MEND	Movement for the Emancipation of the Niger Delta
NDI	National Democratic Institute for International Affairs
NEITI	Nigerian Extractive Industries Transparency Initiative
PEPFAR	President's Emergency Plan for AIDS Relief
PDP	People's Democratic Party
UNDP	United Nations Development Programme
USAID	United States' Agency for International Development

COUNCIL SPECIAL REPORT

AS NIGERIA GOES, SO GOES AFRICA

Nigeria's vital importance for Africa's political development, for U.S. and European interests, and for world order cannot be exaggerated. Nigeria's sheer aggregate numbers—possibly as many as 150 million of the full continent's 800 million—and its proportionate weight in sub-Saharan Africa's troubled affairs, make the country's continuing evolution from military dictatorship to stable, sustained democracy critical.

Moreover, four factors are salient. First, Nigeria's sizable production of petroleum, 3.22 percent of world output and 8.5 percent of all U.S. imports, emphasizes Washington's deep interest in sub-Saharan Africa's most populous country. Second, that Nigeria is a committed Muslim land as well as a fervently Christian polity raises questions about Islamism and potential sanctuaries for global terrorists. So far, however, even if northern Nigerians have expressed views favorable to Islam in public opinion surveys, there has been no known embrace of Islamist terror. Indeed, if encouraged and well led, Nigeria could become an effective example of Muslim-Christian cooperation within a plural nation. Third, from a health security vantage point, HIV/AIDS is ravaging Nigeria, as are malaria and tuberculosis. Avian influenza's reservoirs exist significantly in Nigeria and threaten other countries. Likewise, just as Nigeria's role in exporting polio and measles after failed inoculation campaigns demonstrated, borders no longer bar contagion. What infects Nigerians potentially endangers all of Africa and the world. Fourth, Nigeria has abundant economic potential beyond oil. It is the fastest-growing telecoms market in the world. Its stock market is thriving. Nigerians do not lack for entrepreneurial talent.

But despite oil wealth, despite its vast human capacity, despite its demonstrated heft in the African Union and its significant role in reversing coups in West Africa and helping to broker the Darfurian and other peace initiatives, Nigeria is still a poor, struggling country, even by the standards of its continent. In 2006, Nigeria's gross domestic product (GDP) per capita was $800. That modest figure, less than Mauritania, Côte d'Ivoire, and Senegal, but more than Benin and Ghana, camouflages vast disparities of wealth—Nigeria's Gini coefficient was 0.44 in 2003, among the least equal income spreads in Africa. The Economist Intelligence Unit reports that 70 percent of Nigerians live on less than $1 per day. Nor are Nigeria's social attainments commensurate with its oil and gas wealth. Although $500 billion of oil has been extracted since 1970, life expectancy at birth was only forty-three in 2006, a poor number even within Africa.

These numbers, and Nigeria's reputation as one of the world's most corrupt places, mask the reality that Nigeria, together with South Africa, remains the pivot of Africa. If Nigeria can harness its oil wealth for the good of all of its people, if it can banish (or at least reduce) poverty and squalor, if it can diminish the palpable sense that an overlord class is stripping the people of their rightful shares of prosperity, and if these changes can be funneled into a sustainable effort, then Nigeria can probably become more secure and a strong leader for good in tomorrow's Africa.

Nigerians want that result. So does the rest of Africa and the international community. But there are severe hurdles to overcome before Nigeria can begin to achieve its national potential—namely, holding free, fair, and credible (incident-free would be too much to hope for) national elections this April, institutionalizing the fledgling steps toward improved governance and transparency begun in the past eight years, and delivering a modicum of political goods to its citizens in all parts of the country. Good governance is just that: the provision of adequate qualities and quantities of the prime political goods of security, rule of law, political freedom, economic opportunity, and access to infrastructure, education, health, and an empowered civil society.

As Nigeria approaches these crucial elections and a series of decisions that may well alter the trajectory of democracy there and throughout Africa, it draws on a strong well of recent national political accomplishment. The woes of Nigerians may be many, but so are its achievements as a reconstructed nation-state since 1999, when President Olusegun Obasanjo led the nation back to democracy after decades of excessively corrupt military tyranny. Nigeria and Nigerians have been resilient. There is a large, expanding middle class that cherishes and demands more, rather than less, stability. The ranks of the hegemonic bourgeoisie are expanding; entrepreneurs less and less depend on the largesse of the state. The government's dominance of the economy is shrinking, giving space for

Nigeria's numerous, skillful entrepreneurs to take the initiative within an increasingly participatory framework.

Most of all, Nigeria has demonstrated since 1999 that it can survive the kinds of major crises that would have derailed less secure, less mature polities. As a "secular" state, Nigeria has managed without too much dissonance to endure and embrace the introduction of sharia law into its north. Contentious as was that insertion of religious law, the nation itself never crumbled. The nation also survived another census, historically a source of competition and conflict. Last year's exercise was received with a little less opprobrium than its predecessors in 1962–63, 1973, and 1991, and was endorsed by the Council of State. It was, comparatively, a successful milestone despite ample cries of disdain in the press and from Lagos.

Similarly, Obasanjo's quest for a third presidential term, breaching constitutional provisions, could have rent the national fabric. Instead, the legislative branch of government diffused hostility and anger, denying Obasanjo what he wanted but without pushing the nation into violence. Shifts in political power from north to south and now, potentially, back again, seem to be accepted as normal—a potential affirmation of Nigeria's growing political maturity. Power sharing, in other words, has become a recognized norm.

The professionalism of the higher judiciary, especially the Supreme Court, has by and large been a force for good, and for moderation, at the national level. Important constitutional challenges have been debated and judged there rather than settled in the streets or by coups. Obasanjo's administration has managed to institute improved budgeting practices, begin reforming the banking system, and massively reduce Nigeria's foreign debt. Furthermore, probity in the petroleum sector has been enhanced thanks to the Nigerian Extractive Industries Transparency Initiative (NEITI). Outside of the government, Nigeria has a thriving civil society. Active nongovernmental organizations, and especially a vibrant media, mean that public accountability mechanisms function.

For policymakers everywhere, Nigeria should be *the* central African question. No country's fate is so decisive for the continent. No other country across a range of issues has the power so thoroughly to shape outcomes elsewhere in sub-Saharan Africa. If Nigeria works well, so might Africa. If the democratic experiment in Nigeria stalls, and development and governance stagnate, the rest of Africa suffers and loses hope. This report carefully examines Nigeria's abundant advances since 1999, discusses some of the constraints on further progress, and recommends a range of policy priorities for Abuja, Washington, Brussels, and London in 2007 and thereafter.

In urgent particular, this report argues that Washington should immediately turn policy eyes to Nigerian questions now, in time to help Nigerians to hold democratically confirming elections in April. A presidential-appointed mission or task force is required, together with high-level attention to many of the near-term and medium-term questions set out in this report and in the appended recommendations. A rapid injection of democracy and governance funding is indicated to assist the Nigerian government in strengthening civil society and accountability before, during, and after the election season. Longer term, the United States and other donors should find the means to offer enduring assistance to Nigeria across the range of governance problems specified throughout this report. A high-level forum—a U.S.-Nigeria commission modeled on the U.S.-China, U.S.-India, and U.S.-Brazil commission models—should be established by Congress to encourage regular dialogue between senior American and Nigerian officials and businesspeople.

NATIONAL ELECTIONS

The first and most important challenge facing Nigeria concerns this year's scheduled presidential, parliamentary, and gubernatorial elections in April. It is not so much whether the elections are held on time, with a good turnout, without too much violence, and are seen to be fully fair, although those considerations are obviously important. What matters is whether the election results at the national and state levels contribute to peace, prosperity, and a sense of renewed national purpose. If the electoral results instead ratify the status quo—the existing divisions between north and south, between haves and have-nots, and between power brokers and the powerless—then Nigeria will have passed an electoral test without providing a platform for a forward-looking transformation of attitudes and prospects.

A CREDIBLE CONTEST

In the weeks before the election, few can be sanguine about Nigeria even passing the basic test. A few observers fear, first, that President Obasanjo, who was rebuffed by the National Assembly in 2006 when he sought a constitutional change to permit him to contest a third elected term, will declare an emergency and annul or abort the election. Second, the electoral register only closed in February 2007, months late, without the registrar sounding terribly confident about his ability to produce a reliable list of qualified voters in time for the April poll. About 57 million of perhaps 60 million eligible voters—a credible result if the numbers are accurate—registered despite general apathy and problems with a new computerized system that was hard to operate in an atmosphere of daily power outages across the nation. Absent an acceptable list (or even with one), the election itself will doubtless be marred by legitimate and illegitimate controversies over who should and could vote, and thus over fairness. (A powerful local politician in Ibadan apparently installed six of the voter registration machines inside his own house. And he was not alone.)

There will be reasonable claims that individuals and whole communities have been disenfranchised and/or given unfair advantage, especially in the Igbo-dominated southeast and in the Niger Delta. Violence at the polls must be anticipated in order to discourage classes of voters, too, and in reaction to those real or perceived violations of expectations of fairness. The Independent National Election Commission (INEC) has an officially declared "zero tolerance" for electoral violence, and has threatened to cancel voting in areas where violence occurs, but its policies and actions may have little influence on actual polling experiences.

Attempts to subvert the electoral process by buying votes en masse should be anticipated. If the approximate cost of a race for a state governorship is about $10 million, and for the presidency about $100 million, it is clear that heavy funding can clear fields at all levels and also make national, state, and local candidates slavishly beholden to their backers (as in all recent elections). Candidates will be contesting 109 Senate seats and 360 House of Representatives seats, plus all the governorships—possibly the most bitterly contested and arguably most critical positions—and all the seats in the thirty-six state assemblies. In 2006, Obasanjo's People's Democratic Party (PDP) held seventy-three Senate seats and 221 House seats; the All Nigeria Party held twenty-eight and ninety-four; and the Alliance for Democracy six and thirty-four.

April's election promises, moreover—even by Nigerian standards—to be thoroughly corrupt. At this point, there are few effective mechanisms, not necessarily the INEC or the Economic and Financial Crimes Commission (EFCC), to limit corrupt practices in a society where contests as lucrative as those for elected office are held. In 2006, four state governors were investigated for alleged corruption and money laundering. Four were impeached and forced from office by their states for fraud and peculation (the governors of Anambra, Bayelsa, Ekiti, and Oyo States), and thirty others were suspect, if also envied for their allegedly ill-gotten wealth. A fifth, the governor of Plateau State, had been arrested in Britain in 2004 for money laundering, but jumped bail. In 2006, he, too, was impeached. In early 2007, the governor of Taraba State was also under investigation. Additionally, in 2007, the impeachments ended up in the courts, and one was voided and others were still being adjudicated. Still further appeals were likely.

Despite such adverse possibilities, it is likely that Nigeria will manage to hold an election in April; the country's officials will be able to produce reasonably credible results despite episodes of violence, rigging, vote buying, fabrication, fraud, and polling day mistakes. Reducing such problems, especially allegations of blatant fabrication, to a minimum would contribute to credibility and postelectoral political calm. It would also demonstrate to Africa and the world that democratic practices and values were beginning to take root in the continent's largest and most fractured nation-state. It is not too late for outsiders to contribute to capacity building in this realm by direct assistance in each facet of the larger electoral enterprise.

THE CANDIDATES

The list and apparent quality of the twenty-five or so candidates for president, especially those from the major parties, confirm Nigeria's existing straitjacket, foreshadow few domestic policy changes, and provide little confidence that a new leadership will do more—and be more vigorous and bold than today's leadership—in confronting the country's many formative challenges.

Obasanjo has had the ear and the confidence of Washington and London and is a force in Africa, but he has taken only modest and questionably sustainable steps to improve governance and done little of consequence to address Nigeria's persistent problems of poverty and political alienation. He has done too little to grow Nigeria on the back of its oil wealth, has done less than he might have to rein in corrupt practices despite several notable achievements, has presided over increasing internecine violence in the Niger Delta and throughout the Middle Belt and the North, and, most of all, has accomplished less than he might have in overcoming the nation's long-festering regional enmities and suspicions. Nigeria today is less united and more divisively fractious than it was when Obasanjo (as an army general) and others ruled it militarily in the 1970s and 1980s.

His handpicked successor, the candidate of the PDP, was chosen in late 2006 to confirm entitlements and the political status quo. Precisely because Obasanjo is a

Christian southerner and it was thought to be the turn of a Muslim from the north (power sharing is now an accepted positive virtue), Obasanjo was obligated to his backers (and in order to blunt the demands of northern, Muslim generals and northern, Muslim power brokers and former generals) to anoint a northern successor who would ruffle few feathers and be broadly acceptable within the party and across the north (if not the south).

Alhaji Umaru Musa Yar'Adua fulfills those requirements well. But whether he can be the strong, consensus-building, forward-looking leader that Nigeria desperately needs is much less clear. Little known before his nomination, the colorless, taciturn, fifty-six-year-old Yar'Adua was a self-confessed Marxist undergraduate at Ahmadu Bello University from 1972 to 1975 and outspokenly opposed his prominent elder brother's capitalist tendencies. He received BA and MA degrees from Ahmadu Bello. Later, the younger brother taught chemistry at Katsina College of Arts and Sciences between 1976 and 1979 and at Katsina Polytechnic between 1979 and 1983. He is now governor of Katsina State and one of Nigeria's few governors not being investigated for corruption. Yar'Adua's kidneys failed in 2000, and, after operations in Germany, his health was only partially restored.[1] His father was a cabinet minister in a postindependence government, His late elder brother, Major General Shehu Musa Yar'Adua—the capitalist in question—was deputy president during Obasanjo's first term as national president between 1976 and 1979.

Musa Yar'Adua is renowned for his humility and his ascetic qualities. He is regarded by observers in the north as being mildly authoritarian, as poorly respecting the political opposition in his state, and of having done elaborate favors for Katsina's powerful business elite. He is said to have approved giving contracts to companies with links to his family's vast local banks and industries. Some suspect that he will be a front man for Obasanjo and his close associates, who will continue to run Nigeria after the April election. (Obasanjo will remain "Leader for Life" within the PDP.) Obasanjo is said to have employed a mixture of promises and threats of investigation to persuade ten influential state governors to withdraw from the PDP contest and to back Yar'Adua. "Many disillusioned party members think that Yar'Adua's main usefulness to his patron

---

[1] On March 7, 2007, Yar'Adua was reportedly flown to Germany for further medical treatment. As this report goes to press, Yar'Adua's health—and its impact on the impending contest—remains the subject of speculation. *The Guardian* (Lagos), March 7, 2007.

10

will be to protect his immunity from prosecution after he leaves office."[2] After being nominated, Yar'Adua called Obasanjo the "father of democracy and good governance in Nigeria."

Yet, according to Nigerian journalists close to Katsina and Kaduna politics, Obasanjo may not be able to control his handpicked putative successor. Some suggest that Yar'Adua is sufficiently strong to use Obasanjo's patronage, and the backing of various corrupt factions in Katsina, from now until the election, and then to dump them all later. Yar'Adua built up a strong following among party cadres in the late 1980s and early 1990s. He won the loyalty of younger rank-and-file members by his inner dynamism (masked by that taciturn shell). Unlike his better-connected elder brother, Yar'Adua was a tireless grassroots campaigner and mobilizer. In 1998, after the PDP was formed, Yar'Adua again conducted a campaigning blitz, visiting each of Katsina's thirty-four local governments, often going for days without sleep, according to Mahmud Jega, then of the *New Nigerian Weekly*. In late 2006, during a campaign stop in Damaturu in Katsina State, Yar'Adua used one of his favorite phrases: "Allah gives power to whom He wants at the time He wants."

According to Jega, after Yar'Adua became governor in 1999, he introduced austerity, simplicity, and openness into the state's governance. In a departure from the usual behavior of "big men" in Nigerian and African politics, Yar'Adua served modest food in Government House, eschewed the use of a generator despite frequent power outages, drove his own car, and even prayed under a tree and not in the local mosque alongside the Emir of Katsina. Later, he compelled the state ministry of finance to reveal its accounts on radio and television every month. In 1999 and again in 2003, after being reelected, he declared his own assets, including his two houses. More significantly, he insisted on having sufficient cash in the state treasury before permitting contracts to be awarded. When funds finally accumulated, he improved educational facilities and constructed bridges.

Yar'Adua, with a nod toward national unity and conscious also of continued violence in the petroleum-producing region of the Niger Delta, and the PDP chose Goodluck Ebele Jonathan to be the vice presidential candidate on the PDP ticket. A fifty-

---

[2] *The Economist*, December 23, 2006.

five-year-old Christian Ijaw, Jonathan has governed Bayelsa State only since the end of 2005. Previously an unremarkable deputy governor, he replaced the discredited Diepreye Alamieyeseigha after the latter was charged with money laundering in Britain, jumped bail, returned to Nigeria dressed as a woman, and was subsequently impeached by the state assembly. In 2006, Jonathan's wife was indicted by the national EFCC for money laundering and related offenses. Patience Jonathan, Goodluck Jonathan's wife, is considered by some to be the "greediest person in Bayelsa State."[3] She is also seen as cruel; she ordered the fiancée of a prominent Ijaw leader thrown in a detention center and turned down all pleas to have her released. More positively, she established a foundation to improve the lives of the people in her state and says working for the women of the state is her top priority. Yar'Adua and Jonathan comprise a remarkably weak and potentially compromised pair of candidates. Rank-and-file PDP members had hoped for better, as had the country.

Opposing Yar'Adua and Jonathan (among the major candidates) are Major General Muhammadu Buhari, sixty-four, of the All Nigeria People's Party (backed also by the Conference of Nigeria Political parties and the Nigeria Advance Party) and current Vice President Atiku Abubakar, sixty, who refused to back Obasanjo's attempt to serve a third term and was subsequently ousted from the PDP. He joined the Action Congress. The Court of Appeals decided in 2007 that Obasanjo had improperly dismissed him from the vice presidency in 2006.

Atiku has been accused of diverting $125 million from state coffers to personal businesses. Along with more than 130 other candidates for various offices, Atiku was cited in February 2007 by the EFCC as being potentially ineligible for the electoral contest, undermining his viability as a candidate. Indeed, the INEC said that he could not be a candidate, that he was "unfit." The INEC's disqualification of Atiku was overturned, however, by a Federal High Court in Abuja in early March 2007. The court ruled that while the INEC had the right to verify or screen candidates and fine a political party that presents the name of a candidate who did not meet the qualifications stipulated in Electoral Act of 2006, it lacked the powers to disqualify a candidate from contesting

---

[3] *International Herald Tribune,* September 11, 2006; *Vanguard* (Lagos), March 31, 2006.

election.[4] Subsequently, the INEC said that the disqualification still stood. But the story need not end there.

Buhari, who ruled Nigeria from 1983 to 1985, is from Katsina State, along with Yar'Adua, and is also Fulani. As military ruler, he initiated a war against "indiscipline," which is remembered as successful; about five hundred officials and businessmen were jailed for "waste" and corruption. He also compelled notoriously disorderly Nigerians to queue neatly and quietly for buses. He forced tardy civil servants to do public penance by doing calisthenics. However, he stifled all criticism of his aims and methods, decreeing indefinite detention of opponents without trial and shutting down the press. Buhari himself is not regarded as corrupt. Indeed, Buhari's downfall was precipitated by his determination to investigate the fraudulent manner in which the army had awarded contracts; the coup against him in 1985 was led by General Ibrahim Babangida, sixty-five, who was among those generals implicated in the contracting investigations and who, today, is still a moneyed force in national politics.

Buhari lost to Obasanjo in the presidential contest of 2003 and appealed to the courts for redress rather than taking his followers into the streets. If Babangida deploys his political clout and formidable fortune in favor or Buhari or Atiku, the one chosen could prove a formidable contender, especially in vying for the northern vote. (The wily Babangida, however, has publicly backed Yar'Adua.)

Atiku, a Fulani Muslim, was born in what is now Adamawa State, was orphaned at eight, and nevertheless made his way through the Jada primary school and the Adamawa Provincial Secondary School in Yola. Later he studied for a diploma in tropical medicine at the Kano School of Hygiene and then obtained a diploma in law at Ahmadu Bello University in 1967–68. He was involved in student politics at Ahmadu Bello.

Atiku entered the Nigerian Customs and Excise Service in 1969, rising after twenty years to be its deputy director. Then he became a private businessman, investing in oil, insurance, pharmaceuticals, and agriculture. He also worked closely with Yar'Adua's elder brother in the People's Front for Nigeria. Atiku backed Shehu Yar'Adua as the Social Democratic Party's presidential candidate in 1992. He also

---

[4] *The Guardian* (Lagos), March 8, 2007.

supported the successful candidacy of Chief Moshood K. O. Abiola for president in 1993. Under the Abacha military dictatorship, Atiku led the People's Democratic Movement, and went underground. In 1998, after Abacha's demise, he led the remnants of the People's Democratic Movement into the PDP, with Obasanjo as its leader and candidate. Atiku was chairman of seven companies and the newly elected governor of Adamawa State before being elected vice president on the Obasanjo ticket in 1999.

Despite Jonathan's appearance on the PDP electoral roster, the decisive presidential contest will be among northerners only. Thus, northerners in April will remain masters of Nigeria's destiny despite reasonable attempts under Obasanjo to dilute ethnic/regional hegemony through informal power sharing and creative federalism. Yet, neither of the candidates is a national rather than a sectional leader despite their pretensions to the contrary. Indeed, no potential leader of unquestioned domestic integrity and international stature has emerged to succeed Obasanjo, whose legitimacy was ensured when the regime of President Sani Abacha incarcerated him in 1995.

Since no successor to Obasanjo will have an international following comparable to his or be able to deploy such comparable local standing as a Christian southerner with military (and northern) backers, effective leadership for change will be wanting. Nigeria's already precarious position as a nation-state at risk of failure will therefore become more, rather than less, pronounced. Indeed, since Nigeria under Obasanjo has been troubled, with increasing poles of dissent and separation, the results of the electoral contest—however credible on procedural grounds—may well worsen existing divides and do little to dampen the fires of discontent in the Delta or between supposed indigenes and newcomers in the towns of the Middle Belt. Those are among the worries.

INTERNATIONAL SUPPORT

The United States, the United Kingdom, the UN Development Program (UNDP), and others have been supporting Nigeria's efforts to hold credible national elections and help Nigeria peacefully transition from one civilian president to another. The U.S. Agency for International Development (USAID) budgeted $15 million for a three-year Nigerian election and political processes support program (July 2005–May 2008). The primary vehicle for the delivery of this U.S. assistance has been the Consortium for Elections and Political Processes Strengthening. Its tasks, including enhancing the INEC's capabilities, improving voter education and domestic monitoring programs, and increasing transparency, have been divided among the consortium's partners, the National Democratic Institute for International Affairs (NDI), the International Republican Institute (IRI), and the International Foundation for Election Systems (IFES). International preelection delegations organized by NDI and IRI traveled to Nigeria in 2006 to assess preparations for the 2007 elections, including technical capabilities and the organization of monitors.

The United Kingdom has contributed to election preparation through the "Nigerian Election Support 2007" program. Funded by a £3 million Department for International Development grant, the program is managed by another consortium of international organizations, including the IFES, Global Rights, and the Institute for Democracy in South Africa. Its activities include promoting institutional and political finance reform, providing technical assistance, and advising INEC.

International donors have pooled an additional $30 million in resources in support of the successful conduct of the elections. A joint donor basket fund, managed by UNDP, is providing the INEC with technical assistance, supporting electoral training and staffing and police sensitization programs, and helping to finance civil society organizations' efforts to monitor the contest. Approximately one-fifth of the fund is earmarked for grants to civil society.

Domestic observation of the voting will be conducted by the Transition Monitoring Group, Civil Liberties Organization, and, notably, a cooperative effort between the Christian Association of Nigeria and the Supreme Council on Islamic Affairs. The Alliance for Credible Elections in Nigeria announced its intention to present 240,000 observers (one individual from each organization for each of the country's 120 polling units) for the elections. A plethora of internationals—organized by diplomatic missions and international and regional organizations—will observe the elections alongside domestic monitors.

GOOD GOVERNANCE

Achieving good governance requires that the Nigerian state provide adequate qualities and quantities of the prime political goods of security, rule of law, political freedom, economic opportunity, access to infrastructure, education, health, and empowered civil society.

SECURITY

Thus far (since Obasanjo became Nigeria's civilian president in 1999), Nigeria is remarkably less secure than when he took office. Its external borders are unchallenged, but nonstate actors and a variety of indigenous insurgent groups continue to attack (rather brazenly) either the nation-state or the governments of individual states. The nation-state cannot claim a monopoly on the sources of firepower or violence. Additionally, crime against persons, including murder, rape, and robbery, has grown in scale and viciousness. For instance, a survey conducted in 2005 revealed that 25 percent of respondents in Lagos had been victims of theft at some point in the past five years, 12 percent said they had been assaulted, and 9 percent of women admitted being victims of sexual violence.

The Niger Delta

Violence in the oil lands of the Niger Delta, in the Middle Belt between supposed "natives" and alleged "newcomers," and throughout the whole of the country between Muslims and Christians, continues to threaten Nigeria's national sense of itself and to undermine democracy and development. Oil has flowed from the Niger Delta region since 1970. In the six states of the Niger Delta, seven million Ijaw, Ogoni, Itsekiri, Andoni, Ibibio, and other communities have since about 1980 demanded a greater share of Nigeria's oil and gas wealth than that allotted to the relevant local states, now according to the revenue-sharing provisions of the Constitution of 1999.

The Delta region's energy assets provide about 75 percent of all government revenues from minerals. Under Obasanjo, who served as minister of petroleum resources until the end of 2006 as well as president, the nation talked of various ways to be more generous with regard to oil-derived revenues, and about 13 percent of all national revenues, more than ever before, now flow back to the Delta. Even so, those attempts to return additional monies to the relevant states, and new well-meant federal instruments of transparency and other initiatives, have been derided as too miserly and much too late. Certainly they little appease or deflect from militancy the several locally strong protest movements, the most significant of which nowadays is the umbrella Movement for the Emancipation of the Niger Delta (MEND).

In the Delta, insurgents are battling for local hegemony, for control over oil royalties, for autonomy, and for leverage over both the foreign and domestic petroleum-producing companies that exploit deep petroleum reservoirs onshore amid the creeks and tributaries of the mouth of the Niger River and under the Gulf of Guinea. MEND says that it is fighting for "total control" of the Delta's oil riches since the local people have not gained commensurately from "their" resources and from the despoiling of their domain. They also look around them in the Delta and elsewhere and wonder where Nigeria's ample oil and gas revenues have gone; most of the Delta, and much of the remainder of the vast country, is deeply impoverished, with little access to clean water, electric power, or even good, unpaved roads. Bayelsa State boasts only one multilane, paved road, naturally leading to the state capital. Within the Delta there are few decent hospitals or satisfactory schools and many lack staff, supplies, or equipment. The environmental insults have been damaging and numerous—oil spills, blowouts, fires, sulfuric acid spews, and acid rain—and wellhead natural gas flares that turn day into night as well as release 25 million tons of carbon dioxide and 12 million tons of methane into the air annually.

MEND claims to be a "union of all relevant militant groups in the Niger Delta," some of which are political and some of which are criminal. These groups, notably the criminal ones, finance their protest activities by the dangerous and destructive process of siphoning and selling oil from pipelines, extorting "protection" funds, and kidnapping foreigners for ransom. The criminal gangs have also become major arms importers into the Delta. Some of these gangs are allied to state governors or other politicized factions; the line between protest and criminality is too often blurred.

In late 2006, several sets of foreign oil workers were held for weeks and ransomed for substantial sums. More than one hundred foreign hostages were seized throughout all of 2006; a number of them, as well as others caught in the cross fire, were killed. In early 2007, separate sets of Chinese, Korean, Filipino, Lebanese, and Italian workers were kidnapped. In late February 2007, seven hostages were still being held, twenty-four Filipinos having recently been released. Each attack on foreigners shuts down a pumping station, delaying production and accelerating global anxiety about Nigeria's reliability as an oil exporter. Car bombs planted by MEND in Port Harcourt also added to the general atmosphere of danger and malaise in late 2006. In January 2007, fifty machine-gun firing MEND affiliates attacked the main police station in Port Harcourt, killing a passerby and freeing one of its notorious jailed leaders, a so-called gangster.

The actual number of barrels of oil exported falls each time extractive activities are disturbed by MEND or others. Although Nigeria exported 2.5 million barrels of oil in 2005, the violence of 2006 reduced that total by 25 percent. This year promises to be worse for petroleum production (and therefore for foreign importers), as little national leadership is being exerted to negotiate with the Delta movements or to contain them militarily.

The Delta is a mess, and the failures of state and local governments, plus massive peculation, are at least partially responsible for the destruction and despoliation of the environmental commons and for the mayhem that is among the major stories of the Delta. The police cannot control events there. Military patrols will be essential. What could help address the root causes of unrest and violence would be international participation and independent oversight of a special international fund for the overhaul and uplift of the Delta—as discussed in the recommendations section of this report—plus the exercise of greater responsibility by oil producers. Equally critical at the local level would be the initiation of a viable dialogue between militants and representatives of civil society, and between local rulers (the local elections are apt to be rigged) and genuine representatives of "the people."

SECTARIANISM AND ETHNOLINGUISTIC FRACTIONALIZATION

Sectarian and communal strife in the Delta and throughout the entire nation stems from a lack of credible leadership in Abuja and in the states, and an overemphasis on the politics of personalist rule. The delegitimation of national and state institutions, the perceived absence of formal avenues for political participation by aggrieved groups at all levels, and a federal government that has failed to project power all contribute to the growth in violence.

Furthermore, no one trusts the poorly trained national Nigerian Police Force (NPF), or its local detachments, to provide effective human protection anywhere, whether in the Delta, in Lagos, or in the cities of the north. Minorities justly fear that they will be victimized or oppressed. Sometimes they accordingly react defensively and preemptively. Given the scarcity of alternatives, entities that rightly or wrongly consider themselves disadvantaged seek redress for grievances through local or regional mayhem. Protest surges, vigilante brigades, and intercommunal mayhem then results, more often than not within a cascade of tit-for-tat retribution.

Nigeria, after all, contains more than 250 ethnolinguistic groups and about seventy "nationalities." Hausa, Igbo, and Yoruba speakers account for about 60 percent of the total population, according to the discredited existing censuses, but within each of the thirty-six states and one federal territory, even within the twelve sharia-observant northern states, there are long-resident and recently resident minorities, some ethnolinguistic, some religious, and some a combination of both such identities making and shaking concerns. From its origins as a nation, Nigeria has been unsure and confused about whether legal and administrative institutions of governance should recognize or mostly ignore those distinctions. Nigeria has attempted over its four-plus decades to honor self-determination within a governmental framework much more unitary than federal. Among the many critical issues now facing Obasanjo's successor is whether and how to deal with the continued upwellings of claims to self-determination, as in the Delta, and at the same time improve security for all Nigerians through the exercise of responsible central control.

During Obasanjo's time, Nigeria has been unable to protect its citizens equally. More than 12,000 people have been killed since 1999 in local clashes, and more than three million have been displaced from their homes. Jukun have fought Tiv in the Middle Belt, especially in Taraba State. Yoruba have battled Hausa in the southwest. Christians have fought Muslims in Kaduna, Yelwa, and elsewhere in Plateau State with great losses of life. Igbo have clashed with Hausa in the southeast. Jos, once an oasis of peace, has seen several bitter clashes between supposed indigenous and nonindigenous groups. There has been fighting in Langtang North and South, in Wase, Bardi Ladi, Riyom, and in many other places. Each clash has a specific local cause and a possible local solution. But nearly all of the ongoing conflicts, real or perceived, are over resources. Trading privileges, employment possibilities, welfare payments, water access, and land rights are continually contested.

In the absence of any belief in the legitimacy—and fair dealing—of governmental authority, and given deep skepticism everywhere over local and national rule of law regimes, these intercommunal disputes—and their violent settling—will hardly diminish. A new president and his government could do well to foster a climate of tolerance and equitable resolution, but that might mean rebuilding the NPF and judicial systems from scratch.

Obasanjo could well argue that the governance problem is in the states, not in the nation. After all, the states collectively receive half of Nigeria's oil revenues, and spend those revenues inconsistently and without much accountability. Many of the decisions that affect aggrieved communities adversely are indeed taken at the state level, especially by autocratic governors. When state civil services overwhelmingly employ the members of one ethnolinguistic group over another, confidence is very hard to engender, especially in those states where heterogeneity is the rule. Preferential admission to secondary schools and local universities creates additional grievances. Land ownership is contested. Access to political opportunity may also be limited or circumscribed. Above all, the heavy corruption and partiality of state governors and governments hardly boosts confidence in the overall system among those in the minority or out of favor. Reform of state governance is therefore overdue, but April's election is unlikely to produce a president or legislators capable of restructuring the nation in this manner. Some of the candidates for president in April may or may not transcend their sectional roots and appeal effectively to the Nigerian nation, but most Nigerians will be skeptical and distrustful regardless.

RULE OF LAW

Another obstacle to national unity, for whoever is elected president, is a judicial system that is seen to be ponderous (in both its criminal and civil procedures), partial, prejudiced, and incompletely independent. The country's formal justice system fails to ensure personal safety or secure personal or corporate property. It rarely settles disputes quickly and fairly, compelling too many Nigerians to conclude disputes by force. Arbitrary arrests are common. So is prolonged incarceration without trial—pretrial detainees comprise at least 70 percent of persons held in prisons. The customary and area courts (south and north, respectively) hear most Nigerian cases. They are as characterized by delay as are the formal courts. They often lack due process, are noted for arbitrariness, and are presumed to be corrupt. Rule-of-law breaches are responsible for the rise of vigilantism or private law enforcement.

The failures of the justice system (despite acknowledged successes in the constitutional realm) are also blamed for serious and systematic human rights abuses. Too few ethnolinguistic conflicts have been effectively justiciable in recent years. Indeed, Bronwen Manby concludes that "impunity for the use of violence for political and personal ends has ... been a major contributor to the escalation of ethnic violence." Moreover, justice at all rungs below the federal appellate level is widely believed to be purchasable. Hence, an initial enthusiasm in 2000 and 2001 for the introduction of more certain, more swift codes of justice; Nigeria's twelve northern, Muslim states adopted the sharia one after the other, despite the "secular" provisions of the national constitution. Even there, however, palpably fair and objective justice has largely remained an ideal.

Rule of law, the second most critical political good, particularly in developing societies, continues to be more of an aspiration than a Nigerian reality.

ECONOMIC OPPORTUNITY AND CORRUPTION

Good governance includes the provision of the political good of economic opportunity—the creation of an environment conducive to the maximizing of personal entrepreneurial instincts within an effectively regulated macroeconomic framework. Because Nigeria under Obasanjo has become more open, with inflation held in check in 2006 at 11 percent, an estimated budget deficit of 1.4 percent of GDP in 2007, and GDP growth rates reaching 5 percent in 2005 but falling in 2006 to 4.3 percent, the Nigerian government can be regarded as successful in delivering a more adequate amount of this political good than its misguided predecessors.

But oil and gas are everything, still providing 20 percent of GDP, 65 percent of budgetary revenues, and 95 percent of foreign exchange earnings. In 2005, Nigeria exported $47 billion worth of petroleum and gas.[5] Agricultural and non-oil mineral exports contribute little to Nigeria's GDP, especially when compared to the 1970s. Once a large exporter of food crops, Nigeria must now import most of its food and most of its refined petroleum products. Manufacturing also constitutes much less of the national economy than at independence.

Because it suffers from a weak rule of law performance, Nigeria also often lacks the ability to enforce contracts without resorting to violence. In the late 1990s, Nigeria's effective "tax effort" was among the poorest on the continent. Nigeria's entrepreneurial culture essentially runs wild, still benefiting individual Nigerians but not Nigeria as a whole. Overall, 70 percent of all Nigerians were deemed "poor" in 2004, more than twice as many as in 1981.

Admittedly, the country's long period of military rule still drags down the economy. Obasanjo's first civilian administration tried in some respects to recover ground, but its economic performance was lethargic. Peter M. Lewis suggests that

---

[5] About 54 percent of Nigerian oil exports go to the United States, 10 percent to Brazil.

"policy initiatives or institutional reforms that might have shifted the country's trajectory were wanting."[6] During the second administration, particularly during the thirty-six months that Ngozi Okonjo-Iweala was finance minister, deficits were reduced, statist remnants were removed, and accountability was enhanced. But Nigeria, with so much annual oil and gas revenue, still underperforms its democratic peers on the continent.

Corruption distorts economic priorities and, as a result, greatly diminishes performance and encourages wave after wave of cynicism and emulation. Levels of venal and lubricating corruption are higher than most places in the world. Corruption is a way of life, especially concerning the government; few such acts are not infused with bribe giving and taking. Governors, judges, bureaucrats, police officials, soldiers, and many citizens enrich themselves whenever possible. No road, bridge, or building is built without officials benefiting. Thus, priorities are endlessly distorted, politicians enriched, and the nation consequently impoverished. In 2006, Transparency International's Corruption Perception Index ranked Nigeria 142 of 163 countries, an improvement over previous years, but still lamentable and probably an understatement of reality.

Obasanjo promised in 1999 to clean house. He appointed an anticorruption commission and later created a serious crimes commission. But he made too few public examples of corrupt cabinet ministers, governors, or others. He also seemed to tilt toward the need for party electoral funds and in favor of corrupt cronies when he pushed aside Finance Minister Okonjo-Iweala in 2006. Yet, in 2006, during the run-up to the next election, there were several prosecutions of prominent miscreants, including several governors, and many threats to expose the corrupt activities of persons opposed to Obasanjo and the PDP. For various reasons, Obasanjo seemed finally to regard combating corruption as an area where he could lead by example.

Yar'Adua may be significantly less corrupt than alternative candidates, especially if his press can be believed, but many of his associates in Katsina are immensely wealthy and his family businesses have always benefited from a gubernatorial connection. He would have to be an extremely strong candidate to run for the presidency with few commitments to wealthy power brokers. He would be unusual for a Nigerian politician if

---

[6] Peter M. Lewis, "Getting the Politics Right: Governance and Economic Failure in Nigeria," in Robert I. Rotberg, ed., *Crafting the New Nigeria: Confronting the Challenges* (Boulder, CO: 2004), p. 121.

he ran an austere campaign or failed to protect himself from being outspent by his opponents. Jonathan also seems potentially tainted, as well as being undistinguished. The PDP team thus enters the final weeks of the electoral season with few claims to unusual integrity and precious little national appeal.

SPREADING THE WEALTH AND COMBATING HIV/AIDS

Historically, Nigeria's wealth has benefited the few, mostly military officers from the north, and their clients. Sticky fingers appropriated billions of dollars; only a matter of millions has been reclaimed from Swiss banks despite determined efforts by the Nigerian and European authorities.

The erosion, and personal appropriation, of state revenues and royalties from oil must explain Nigeria's appalling ranking on every international official and unofficial human development indicator. The 2006 Human Development Index (HDI) prepared by the UNDP ranks Nigeria 159 of 177 countries, after Eritrea and Rwanda, and before Guinea and Angola.[7]

Life expectancy has fallen to forty-three from recent levels in the fifties. Infant mortality rates, for example, are listed as more than ninety-seven per one thousand live births. For comparison, South Africa's rate is fifty-four, Tunisia's is twenty-one, Singapore's is three, Finland's is three, and the U.S. rate is seven. The maternal mortality ratio per one hundred thousand live births in 2000 was eight hundred, among the highest in Africa. About 30 percent of all children under five were underweight for age or height in 2003, an average result for Africa but high compared to Asia or Europe. For instance, countries classified by the World Bank as "middle income" had a malnutrition prevalence of 19 percent height-for-age and 11 percent weight-for-age.

In 2004, there were twenty-seven physicians per one hundred thousand people. In 2001, Nigeria spent an amount equal to 2.6 percent of its GDP on health care, both public and private. Those modest numbers mask a massive drain of medical professionals and

---

[7] HDI measures life expectancy, educational attainment and literacy, adjusted real income, and standards of living.

infrastructural weaknesses that are common to Africa and Nigeria and that work against the new, welcome, external high-profile assistance available to attack the causes of Nigeria's penetrating health problems and virulent diseases.

Neither the national nor the state governments has managed effectively to catch up with and manage the country's very serious HIV/AIDS epidemic. After India and South Africa, Nigeria has the greatest number of HIV/AIDS sufferers in the world. Although its 6 percent adult prevalence rate is far less than the prevalence rate throughout southern and eastern Africa, Nigeria's large population means that at least eight million must be infected in 2007. A few years ago, Daniel J. Smith reported that 170,000 Nigerians died each year from AIDS or AIDS-related diseases.[8] That number reached 220,000 deaths in 2005. Cumulatively, 1.7 million people or so have died since the scourge of HIV/AIDS appeared in 1986, and more than 1.5 million children have been orphaned.

For the country's 2007–11 government, the projections are dire: The adult prevalence rate will reach as high as 26 percent and up to fifteen million people will be infected. By 2011, possibly ten million Nigerians will have died from AIDS. Sometime between now and 2011, Nigeria will overtake South Africa as the continent's most AIDS-devastated nation. Nothing will stanch the trajectory of the disease before 2011, but a fuller distribution of antiretroviral cocktails will enable many sufferers to live longer, and an existing health infrastructure more robust than today's could provide welcome palliative care. But the big challenge is slowing the spread of HIV/AIDS. The Obasanjo government did less than it might have to create governmental programs to combat AIDS and prevent future generations from succumbing.

The U.S. President's Emergency Plan for AIDS Relief (PEPFAR)'s several grants to Nigerian agencies may help to stem the tide of disease, and Nigerians are much more aware now than they were earlier in this century about the spread of AIDS and its economic and social consequences for the nation. But the new Nigerian administration will want to do even more, and to devote increasing proportions of its oil revenues to a massive attack on the disease. The increase in funding should be focused on prevention

---

[8] Daniel J. Smith, "HIV/AIDS in Nigeria: the Challenges of a National Epidemic," in Rotberg, *Nigeria,* p. 200.

efforts. Malaria, tuberculosis, infantile paralysis, and a host of other diseases, including measles and meningococcal fevers, are also rife. The new government, with its northern credibility, needs to do more than the Obasanjo regime did in this general area to explain the necessity of vaccination and other broad spectrum campaigns against such scourges. More of Nigeria's resources, with appropriate help from outside, should be devoted to the ongoing battle against dangers to the health of the nation, the continent, and the globe.

Terrible numbers testify to vast unmet public health needs. In 2003, there were 2,608,479 reported malaria cases and 5,343 reported malaria deaths in Nigeria. In 2004, Nigeria had the world's fourth-largest tuberculosis burden, with nearly 374,000 estimated new cases annually.[9] Of the new and old cases, about 105,000 die annually; the in-country case detection and treatment success rates were among the lowest of nations with high tuberculosis case numbers. In 2004, two-thirds of all polio cases worldwide occurred in Nigeria (760 out of 1,170 total). Between January and August 2004, at least 35,856 children in Nigeria became infected with measles. However, in 2005, Nigeria completed Africa's largest measles campaign, vaccinating thirty million children. In 1996, a meningitis epidemic swept the country, infecting over one hundred thousand people. In 2003, there were 3,508 reported cases, with 428 deaths.

In three countries in the world—Nigeria, Egypt, and Indonesia—the lethal H5N1 avian influenza is officially, by World Health Organization standards, "out of control." A woman (and possibly her relatives) died in crowded Lagos in early 2007 from this flu, demonstrating an alarming human susceptibility. Evidence of the flu in birds has been found in nineteen of Nigeria's thirty-six states, according to the Food and Agriculture Organization. Although Nigeria has already culled about seven hundred thousand domestic chickens and ducks, the president of the national Animal Science Association said that bans on the movement of poultry and the killing of infected birds were not being enforced. Chicken parts, guinea fowl, ducks, and turkeys from northern Nigeria were easily available in southern Nigerian markets in February 2007. Nigeria also exports poultry to all of West Africa. Experts worry that the avian flu could combine with human influenza strains in Nigeria. If so, a pandemic of alarming proportions could follow.

---

[9] World Health Organization, *WHO Report 2006: Global Tuberculosis Control: Surveillance, Planning, Financing*, WHO/HTM/TB/2006.362 (Geneva, 2006).

Nigeria's new government needs to attend to these dangers as well as to strengthen its existing inadequate public health infrastructure.

Although 68 percent of Nigerians are literate, the net primary enrollment ratio was only 67 percent in 2003. The net secondary enrollment ratio, an even more important statistic, was 29 percent in the same year. In Africa, those are below-average attainments. So are all of the comparisons between women and men, with the former considerably lower than men on all measures.

All Nigerians complain about their roads, and access to them. On a universal pothole index, Nigeria's arteries would rate among the worst maintained. For a country the size of two Californias, there are only 60,000 kilometers (km) of nominally paved roads and another 134,000 km of unpaved roads and tracks. California, for comparison, has 169,906 miles (273,437 km) of public roads. Nigerians would welcome attention to their insufficient network of roads, but there are many other critical infrastructural deficits, each of which limits economic growth and democratic achievement.

POLICY RECOMMENDATIONS

The international community—particularly the United States, United Kingdom, and EU—must immediately focus attention on Nigeria in time to help Nigerians hold a democratically confirming election in April. Longer term, the United States and other donors should find the means to offer enduring assistance to Nigeria across the range of governance problems specified throughout this report.

THE ELECTION

Nigeria's 2003 vote was marred by innumerable instances of fraud, rigging, miscounting, and general misfeasance. Because Nigeria's stability and growth as a democracy will be assisted by a more free election in 2007, the United States, EU, United Kingdom, and all well-meaning Nigerians should employ every possible kind of influence on Nigerian officials to ensure the holding of credible elections on schedule in April.

- The U.S. executive branch, and leadership in other donor states, should focus on Nigerian politics and preelection preparation in the weeks approaching the April contest and be prepared to inject rapid assistance to help ensure successful elections. Nigerians should accept such assistance without it reflecting upon or diminishing Nigeria's fundamental responsibility for the oversight and smooth functioning of the electoral process.

- Washington should talk quietly and decisively to President Obasanjo about the strong American preference for elections that are as free and fair as humanly possible. Obasanjo will have the preeminent power to discourage disarray and fraud, but he may not give priority to the same outcome. Because Washington cannot exert strong pressure on Obasanjo or threaten to punish Nigeria if the elections are less than free and fair according to world standards, it may be necessary to employ unusual degrees of diplomatic finesse and to remind

Obasanjo about his legacy in Nigerian history. President George W. Bush and Secretary of State Condoleezza Rice need to act decisively and personally. Time is of the essence.

- Every effort must be made by Nigerians to prevent violence marring the run-up to the polls and the polling days themselves. Since the police cannot be expected to handle myriad incidents of violence themselves, the army should be deployed, but only under strict orders and controls since the army will be suspected of being allied to the PDP. The Delta is a critical area requiring such deployment.

- International observers should arrive well before the April 14 (gubernatorial and state assembly) and April 21 (general) election dates and stay beyond the actual polling day, at least until all the votes are counted and results are verified. International observers should be supportive of Nigerian monitoring efforts, Nigerians safeguarding the integrity of the electoral proceedings, and the subsequent reporting and counting of votes by Nigerians. The international contingent should share all of their observations with the Nigerians so that the latter can employ such data in proceedings before local tribunals (which will be numerous) immediately after the polls.

- Because corruption remains a major stain on Nigeria's reputation and on its democratic performance, the EFCC and INEC should be encouraged to investigate and take to court any and all allegations of corrupt dealings, especially in the weeks before the election. Charges should be pressed as soon as possible—the higher the profile, the better—in order to attempt to limit the spread of bribery and fraud.

- Washington, Brussels, and London should encourage and monitor transparency and evenhandedness of the EFCC and INEC as there is a danger that both commissions have and will target PDP opponents.

Nigeria is fundamentally insecure. Part of the problem is the continued existence of local militias, vigilante groups, protection racketeers, criminal gangs, and so on, many loyal to discredited state governors and other power brokers. Disarming and demobilizing these entities will take major acts of courage and significant exercises of national firepower. If not now, the new Nigerian president should make doing so among his first priorities. Flexing official muscles in this way will greatly contribute—long term—to the enhancement of Nigeria's democracy, to human rights improvements, and to the enlargement of peace and order.

Before such steps can be taken in places like the Niger Delta, however, a demonstrated official willingness to deal with some, if not many, of the legitimate grievances of the peoples of the Delta will be essential. The existing recommendations of the audit of Nigeria's oil and gas sector from 1999–2004 should be employed to ensure transparency and compliance with their obligations by the petroleum-exploiting companies.

- The new Nigerian president should launch an investigation of the role and practices of the Delta Development Commission, with potential dissolution of the commission an option.
- The Nigerian government should create a new community-administered investment fund to invest in projects relevant to and approved by the affected local districts and peoples. Such a fund could oversee the environmental rejuvenation (if that is not too grand a concept) of the Delta and create methods of compensating particularly affected communities. Some form of international oversight of the fund could help ensure its widespread acceptability in the Delta and in Nigeria.

The antidote to violent conflict—and the growth of or sympathy for Islamist-related terror cells anywhere, especially in such regions as the Muslim north—is strengthened democratic performance by the states as well as by the nation, an enhanced criminal justice system, better governance, and massive job creation. Nigeria must take the lead, but outsiders can help in all of those areas, and must do so.

Law and Order

The new government of Nigeria should listen to Nigerian advocates or supplement what is already being said by employing outside consultants to address questions concerning proper law-and-order maintenance within the country.

The current national policing system has many critics and many deficiencies, including a poor human rights record and an absence of independent mechanisms to investigate police abuses and make referrals to prosecutors. USAID's analysis and work on police reform in Nigeria was phased out along with Office of Transition Initiatives efforts there in late 2001. The U.S. Department of Justice's International Criminal Investigative Training Assistance Program (ICITAP), however, continues to operate in Nigeria, working with the government in Kaduna to improve cooperation between police and communities and starting a new national training program for investigating trafficking-in-persons crimes. Although this work is crucial for Nigeria's successful democratic development, U.S. assistance for civil security reform and institutional development is woefully underfunded. For example, the ICITAP budget for Nigeria—currently funded at $400,000 for 2007—should be substantially increased. Likewise, attention should be paid to the judicial system, namely improving integrity, reducing corruption, creating greater timeliness, and reducing the awaiting-trial problem.

- The incoming Nigerian executive and legislature should establish a National Judicial Commission to investigate and modify the judicial institutions, which have to date been a major stain on Nigeria's democratic performance, into an institution capable of upholding the rule of law. Outsiders should encourage and assist such a commission.

- Longer term, improving the training, capacity, and professionalism of Nigeria's police forces should be a larger priority for the U.S. Mission to Nigeria. The U.S. Embassy should discuss with Nigeria the possibility of expanding police institutional development and training programs through ICITAP. Specifically, new programming could include police "accountability" training to help tackle ethics and corruption problems within the police force, election security and civil disturbance techniques, and academy development. Furthermore, the U.S. government should coordinate its civilian law enforcement development initiatives with EU efforts.

- President Obasanjo, or the incoming president, should find a way to reduce the number of government officials constitutionally immune from prosecution (by excluding from immunity everyone other than the president himself) in order to improve the national climate of transparency and integrity.

Democratic Development

Beyond holding credible national elections this year, Nigeria's next administration will be responsible for institutionalizing the fledgling steps toward improved governance and transparency begun in the past eight years and better delivering adequate qualities and quantities of the political goods of rule of law, political freedom, economic opportunity, and access to infrastructure, education, and health. To assist, the donor community needs quickly to find more resources to support Nigeria's democratization and governance process, and future electoral activities.

For example, in advance of the 2007 national elections, the United States programmed only $15 million over three years (2005–07) for democracy support in Nigeria—a virtually inconsequential sum in contrast to the $25 million in support for the 1994 South Africa election alone. The strategic and symbolic importance of Nigeria's democratic experiment demands greater attention and resources moving forward. Excluding the $269 million allocated to Nigeria by PEPFAR, the United States, through USAID, is spending only approximately $50.7 million in 2007 on developmental assistance to Nigeria. Of that, only $15 million supports the objective of "governing justly and democratically." [10] Much more could and should be found for helping build strong Nigerian political institutions.

- External encouragement should be brought upon the Nigerian Senate to pass the laws that would institutionalize reform, such as the NEITI law, the proposed mining law, and the Fiscal Accountability Act.
- Longer term, Washington should focus its funding on the building of strong Nigerian political institutions. For example, beyond the upcoming elections, it will be important to insulate the INEC and other oversight agencies from executive or legislative interference and to ensure that they are funded properly outside the normal budgetary process.

Crucial Health and Infrastructural Issues

Nigeria has tremendous resource wealth. Yet HIV/AIDS, malaria, tuberculosis, and other diseases—and avian flu—promise to overwhelm the country's capacity and its economic and political security unless concerted internal and external efforts are funded and mounted to limit the rapid spread of these epidemics; borders are no barriers to their rapid dissemination. Furthermore, Nigeria's wealth has not translated into reliable, well-maintained infrastructure, inhibiting development and fueling unrest.

- Nigeria's next president should fund anti-HIV efforts much more thoroughly than at present.

---

[10] In 2006, Nigeria received an estimated $41.7 million, of which $8.3 million went toward the "governing justly and democratically" objective. That same year, PEPFAR assistance to Nigeria exceeded $141 million. All figures are from USAID.

- Washington, London, Brussels, and international institutions such as the Global Fund to Fight AIDS, Tuberculosis, and Malaria should do even more than at present to strengthen Nigeria's health care infrastructure.

- The new Nigerian government should focus its infrastructural development efforts on improving the supply of electricity and constructing and maintaining roads. Providing incentives within a tightly regulated framework for the private provision of these essential requirements may offer a fast way forward. The existing Electric Power Sector law may not offer sufficient inducements.

- Domestic oil prices need to be effectively deregulated and new refineries constructed. (A severe shortage of gasoline paralyzed Abuja in early 2007.)

- The United States should establish a major program, to include the Departments of State, Agriculture, Commerce, and USAID, to resuscitate Nigeria's now moribund agricultural sector. Such a program should include efforts to encourage investment in Nigeria's agribusiness sector, increase funding for assistance programs, and expand partnership opportunities for American companies working in Nigeria.

LEADERSHIP

Acting in any of the controversial areas described earlier will test Nigeria's leaders severely. How the new president and his close associates meet such challenges will greatly influence the extent to which Nigeria over the next four years grows democratically and economically or, inexorably, slides back into the abyss of nation-state failure that engulfed the country under Abacha and his immediate predecessors.

- The new president should lead by example, as Yar'Adua did in Katsina, and publicize his personal assets and compel members of his cabinet and all governors to do the same on an annual basis.

Outsiders—friendly Western and African governments and international institutions—can influence these outcomes far less than Nigerians. Nonetheless, Washington now is too distant. Nigeria is too important to be allowed to flounder and fester, and to infect the rest of Africa with any undemocratic malaise. Fully engaged dialogues will be essential and beneficial. So will diplomatically inserted kinds of advice and assistance.

- The United States needs to create a task force, commission, or some similar mechanism—perhaps modeled on several existing effective U.S. national bilateral commissions—to monitor and manage the critical relationship with Nigeria over at least the medium term.

The upcoming gubernatorial and presidential elections in Nigeria provide a decisive opportunity for Nigerians to take another step toward democratic development and good governance. With the close attention and friendly assistance of Washington, London, Brussels, and other donors, the Nigerian government can strive to ensure that the elections are as free and fair as possible. If elected on the basis of a credible and legitimate mandate, the new Nigerian president will be in a strong position to begin to tackle the many problems of corruption, poverty, income distribution, insecurity, and disease that still plague Nigeria. A positive future for Nigeria will not only benefit its own people, but also contribute to the well-being of Africa and the world.

ABOUT THE AUTHOR

Robert I. Rotberg is director of the Program on Intrastate Conflict and Conflict Resolution at the Belfer Center for Science and International Affairs at the Kennedy School of Government, Harvard University. He is also the president of the World Peace Foundation. He was previously a professor of political science and history, Massachusetts Institute of Technology; academic vice president, Tufts University; and president, Lafayette College. He is member of the Council on Foreign Relations and a fellow of the American Academy of Arts and Sciences.

He is the author and editor of numerous books and articles on U.S. foreign policy, Africa, Asia, and the Caribbean, most recently *Building a New Afghanistan* (2007); *Battling Terrorism in the Horn of Africa* (2005); *Crafting a New Nigeria: Confronting the Challenges* (2004); *When States Fail: Causes and Consequences* (2004); and *State Failure and State Weakness in a Time of Terror* (2003).

MISSION STATEMENT OF THE CENTER FOR PREVENTIVE ACTION

The Center for Preventive Action seeks to help prevent, defuse, or resolve deadly conflicts around the world and to expand the body of knowledge on conflict prevention. It does so by creating a forum in which representatives of governments, international organizations, nongovernmental organizations, corporations, and civil society can gather to develop operational and timely strategies for promoting peace in specific conflict situations. The center focuses on conflicts in countries or regions that affect U.S. interests, but may be otherwise overlooked; where prevention appears possible; and when the resources of the Council on Foreign Relations can make a difference. The center does this by:

- *Convening Independent Preventive Action Commissions* composed of Council members, staff, and other experts. The commissions devise a practical, actionable conflict-prevention strategy tailored to the facts of the particular conflict.

- *Issuing Council Special Reports* to evaluate and respond rapidly to developing conflict situations and formulate timely, concrete policy recommendations that the U.S. government, international community, and local actors can use to limit the potential for deadly violence.

- *Engaging the U.S. government and news media* in conflict prevention efforts. The center's staff and commission members meet with administration officials and members of Congress to brief on CPA's findings and recommendations; facilitate contacts between U.S. officials and critical local and external actors; and raise awareness among journalists of potential flashpoints around the globe.

- *Building networks with international organizations and institutions* to complement and leverage the Council's established influence in the U.S. policy arena and increase the impact of CPA's recommendations.

- *Providing a source of expertise on conflict prevention* to include research, case studies, and lessons learned from past conflicts that policymakers and private citizens can use to prevent or mitigate future deadly conflicts.

CENTER FOR PREVENTIVE ACTION ADVISORY COMMITTEE

RECENT COUNCIL SPECIAL REPORTS
SPONSORED BY THE COUNCIL ON FOREIGN RELATIONS

The Economic Logic of Illegal Immigration
Gordon H. Hanson; CSR No. 26, April 2007
A Maurice R. Greenberg Center for Geoeconomic Studies Report

The United States and the WTO Dispute Settlement System
Robert Z. Lawrence; CSR No. 25, March 2007
A Maurice R. Greenberg Center for Geoeconomic Studies Report

Bolivia on the Brink
Eduardo A. Gamarra; CSR No. 24, February 2007
A Center for Preventive Action Report

After the Surge: The Case for U.S. Military Disengagement from Iraq
Steven N. Simon; CSR No. 23, February 2007

Darfur and Beyond: What Is Needed to Prevent Mass Atrocities
Lee Feinstein; CSR No. 22, January 2007

Avoiding Conflict in the Horn of Africa: U.S. Policy Toward Ethiopia and Eritrea
Terrence Lyons; CSR No. 21, December 2006
A Center for Preventive Action Report

Living with Hugo: U.S. Policy Toward Hugo Chávez's Venezuela
Richard Lapper; CSR No. 20, November 2006
A Center for Preventive Action Report

Reforming U.S. Patent Policy: Getting the Incentives Right
Keith E. Maskus; CSR No. 19, November 2006
A Maurice R. Greenberg Center for Geoeconomic Studies Report

Foreign Investment and National Security: Getting the Balance Right
Alan P. Larson, David M. Marchick; CSR No. 18, July 2006
A Maurice R. Greenberg Center for Geoeconomic Studies Report

Challenges for a Postelection Mexico: Issues for U.S. Policy
Pamela K. Starr; CSR No. 17, June 2006 (web-only release) and November 2006

U.S.-India Nuclear Cooperation: A Strategy for Moving Forward
Michael A. Levi and Charles D. Ferguson; CSR No. 16, June 2006

Generating Momentum for a New Era in U.S.-Turkey Relations
Steven A. Cook and Elizabeth Sherwood-Randall; CSR No. 15, June 2006

Peace in Papua: Widening a Window of Opportunity
Blair A. King; CSR No. 14, March 2006
A Center for Preventive Action Report

To purchase a printed copy, call the Brookings Institution Press: 800-537-5487.
Note: Council Special Reports are available to download from the Council's website, CFR.org.
For more information, contact publications@cfr.org.

www.ingramcontent.com/pod-product-compliance
Lightning Source LLC
Chambersburg PA
CBHW081724270326
41933CB00017B/3291